Your children are not your children.
They are the sons and daughters of Life's longing for itself.
They come through you but not from you,
And though they are with you yet they belong not to you.

-   Kahlil Gilran

I0390605

FAMILY AND HELPING HANDS

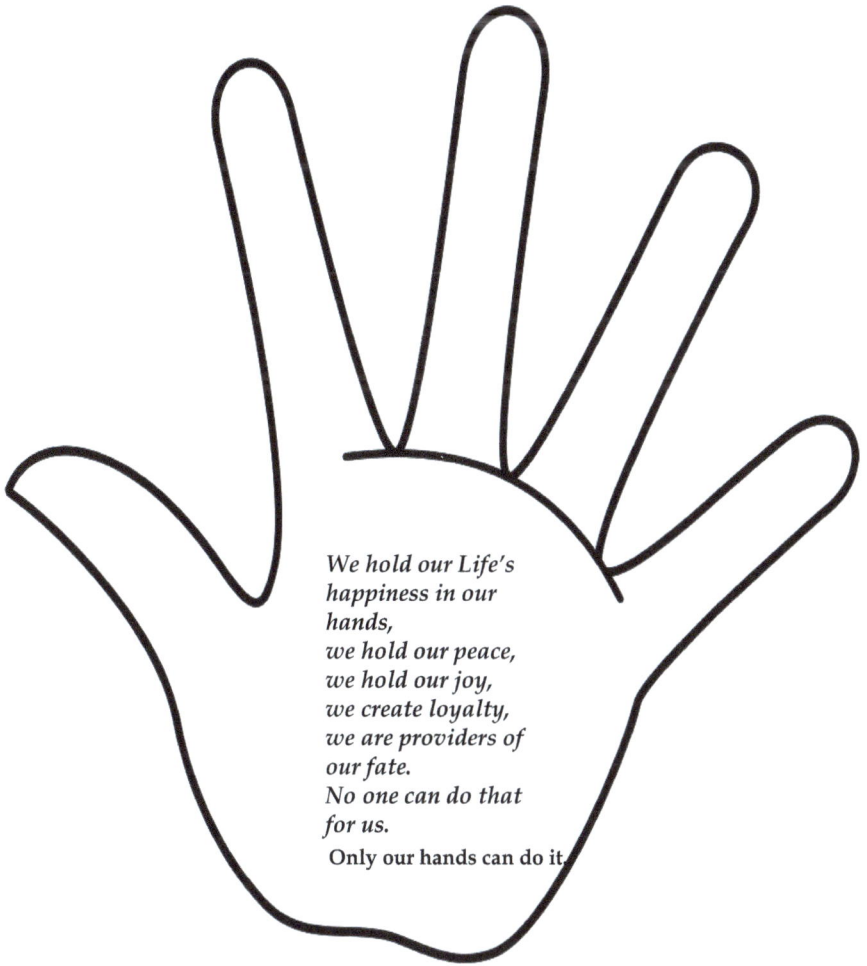

We hold our Life's
happiness in our
hands,
we hold our peace,
we hold our joy,
we create loyalty,
we are providers of
our fate.
No one can do that
for us.
Only our hands can do it.

We must put our hands to work. Who are you giving your hand to help?
Let the Opportunity of Experiencing others Excite you, life will be more
rewarding. Every moment is worth having, if you're living through it.

- The happy Bug

Tribute to
יהוה

I'd like to dedicate this page, a special page to Thank יהוה for being my peace.

Toda יהוה I Love You

יהוה תודה
אני אוהב אותך

Definition Page

This page gives a simple explanation of some words that might not be clear to the reader, and to explain why some words are used.

Yahweh – God יהוה

Ema-   Mother (In Hebrew) אמא

Aba-   Father (in Hebrew) אבא

Toda-   Thank you (in Hebrew) תודה

I love you-   אני אוהב אותך

Throughout this book you'll find that some of my pieces you'll see that I used understand, and in some you'll see overstand that's because through the process of my learning new things I change my verbiage. I just want to leave you with something, we Underestimate, under evaluate but when we get it, we understand. So, I changed the way I acknowledge my overstanding. Hope you have a great experience reading my book.

Love,

The happybug

The happy Bug

Preface

Listening Is The Art Of Paying Attention is a compilation of the thoughts of a woman who has found liberation by writing down her thoughts and through sharing her experiences of how she liberated others. Through the process of learning we discover how much of our strength is drawn from those around us.

As women we feel like we get the short end of the stick and that we're left with a lot to carry on life's plate. It is not uncommon for us to bear the weight of our issues, our children's issues and our man's issues, if we're lucky to have a good man. We are always expected to have such strong backs, it is often not received well when we feel the need to display our emotions. When our burdens become too heavy, we must be mindful of how we express our discomfort lest we be labeled difficult and bitter.

Though I am sure men have a laundry list of valid grievances, I can only speak from my personal experience. This book is in no way intended to trivialize what men endure on a daily basis. I hope I speak for countless woman when I say men, we appreciate and honor you. We need you to know that. I express this with the belief that if you know what it means for a woman to have a good man, perhaps more of you would focus on becoming better versions of yourselves. Let's continue to create families and become greater at being us so that we can create and build them strong. My mission in life is to express to others that they are not alone and to show how important it is to share their experiences.

I hope that you find some peace within the text of this book and maybe some freedom can be extended to you as well

From my heart to yours
Love,

The happy Bug

The happy Bug

Dedication

I dedicate this book to life for happening, for being present, for extending me all the opportunities that could afford me this freedom to write my thoughts. The thoughts that have liberated me and the gift to share myself has freed me enough to help liberate others from themselves. I am grateful for the opportunity to share my gift with others to let them know that they are not alone on this journey called life.

I am thankful to the families that come around my life that has shown me some of the situations that I am so able to freely speak about. I write both from personal experience and from other people's experiences.

I'd also like to dedicate this book to my Ema, she was the guiding force of nature for me. She helped me find my peace in writing; she told me I was the writing portion of my Aba. Ema said that I often sound like aba in my writings and when I speak, she said I have a way of making people want to listen to me. The most amazing thing ema could have ever done for me was let me live in my truth. The most beautiful thing people often tell me is that I have an innate way of making people overstand, and that they stop to listen to what I have to say each time I open my mouth.

I hope this book bring your life some liberty as writing it have brought me mine.

Love
The Happy Bug

The Happy Bug

To: My children,

Daveed, Gabriel, Tamira, Shamirah and Bathsheba; it has been my life's mission to be present for each of you. You have impacted my life in a way unexplainable; I absolutely love each of your dearly. I can't fathom life without the gifts that life so single handedly offered me the moment I became Ema. I have focused on each of you from the moment you come through the stargate into life.

I know at times I might seem crazy when I'm having moments yelling and screaming out of life's frustration but trust me, I really do love each of you freely and passionately. I am always focusing on being the best Ema because you guys are always being the best children. I would like to take this moment to say Thank you for choosing me as your Ema, I would never have been able to hand pick either of you as my children.

I am working to be sure, that the journey you're on is valued here on earth with me. I Thank Yahweh each day for releasing you to my care. May this life continue to bring exactly what you journeyed here for. May I make each of you as proud as you have made me.

I love you always and forever,
Your Ema

The happy Bug

SPECIAL THANKS

To: My Brother Abraham,

I would like to start by saying how much I love you, and how endearing your help has been making my book cover a wonder. You absolutely gave me life. I have found immense peace in working with you during this creative process. Thank you, Abraham, I am eternally grateful for you sharing your gift of artistry and dedicating your time to my project.

I know it is not easy producing something from scratch, and even more difficult developing it from someone's else's mind. Here's the kicker, possessing that ability to do so is profound.

I once I had a premonition that I thought was simple. In this premonition my Aba's children would showcase their inherited talents of Aba's innate ability to be a master jack of all trades. My Aba passed at a very young age. I find it beautiful that all of his children individually create the whole him.

HATS Brother I can't thank you enough. I'd like to take this moment to say I Love You forever and always. May Yahweh continue to guide your heart, may all your endeavors bring you success, may all your goals and dreams take you to the highest level and may you receive more grand opportunities.

Your Big sister Bathsheba
From my heart to yours,

Love,
The happyBug
The happy Bug

Forward

Greetings. My name is Wonderous Horace. I have had the privilege of knowing Bathsheba Israel as both my cousin and best friend all my life. Sheba has been richly blessed with the gift of reaching others through her spoken word and with the power of the pen. To know Bathsheba is to love her.

As someone with first-hand experience, Bathsheba's knowledge and understanding regarding the subject matter outlined in this publication make it a must read. People from all walks of life will find it most helpful and entirely relatable on many levels.

I am honored to be a part of this project because I feel it will educate and repair so many broken individuals and families. This book was created to bridge gaps. May you find hope and healing within these pages.

In Love and Light,

Wonderous Horace

Highlights

Abraham	Artist
Navin	Cover Designer
Wonderous	Editor
Shatory	Strengthener
Crystal	Strengthener

I would like to Thank Navin my graphic designer for always being willing to help me dream. A special Thank you for helping me dream and bringing all my dreams to life.

Love,

The happy Bug

The happy Bug

Vow to Poetry

Life is in itself an experience I work overtime to make the best of, even when it's not clear. I work overtime to make light of every situation both good and bad, I enjoy moments in bad situations and created better moments in good situations because it's necessary to smooth out rough moments along the path, that we will inevitably take. I smile even when there is no joy to have, I write out all my pain, my pen and my paper is my greatest friend. I don't have to worry about any backlash. My paper allows me to be free, I can use any language without someone getting offended, not even my style matters. I can tell my paper using my pen little secrets and don't have to worry about anything even leaking until someone chooses to read it. Behind my pen, I feel safe, behind my pen I feel secure.

So, one day after deeply thinking about this I made a vow to poetry. I made a vow to poetry that I would always use its purpose to reach people, I would use its purpose to emancipate people, and let them know that they are not alone on the path that they find themselves on. My vow to poetry is to always stay true to its will of Freedom and allow those around me to know that it's because of poetry that I am Free. My vow to poetry is to always put it behind my Pen.

May you find peace and happiness for life.

From my heart to yours,

Love,
The happyBug

The happy Bug

Dear Men,

It might not always seem like you're appreciated and by many you might not be. There are some woman who really appreciate you for being the man you are. It might seem to be unfortunate to many people and probably BS that we were put here for the sake of one another and for the sake of things being right. It is our duty to embrace life's purpose by finding where we fit into life. The issue that many of us have is that we haven't been gracious about finding our purpose, therefore we will be unable to really find our peace because we haven't been gracious in doing so. This book is about dysfunctions family dynamics family issues, family secrets and families disfunctions. How well women and men get along will determine how well the family dynamics come together and how well our children prosper and grow. My goal with this gift of information is to reach the reader in a way that changes their thought process or that inspires them to give this book to someone else for their purpose with the hopes that they'd find something that will better themselves in a small piece or in a whole way. Although some of the pieces displayed in this book will seem like male bashing, please know and overstand that this is simply just the experience of the writer and her association with other woman and is not at all any attempt to demean men or discredit men in any way. Your position can't be taken or replaced, I love people in a way that I wish to reach them deep within themselves and change something super simple that will make a big impact on them or someone around them. I pray that this book finds the reader in a great place and in a peaceful place. I pray this book can aid in the beauty of the moment. My heart is clear to be with yours and if your heart is not at ease, I pray you can find a piece of my heart's peace. I leave with you my love.
From my heart to yours,

Love,

The happyBug

The happy Bug

Dear Women,

Our jobs just begin each time we change relationships and each time bear seeds called children.

How we deal with that is determined by the type of woman each of us is. Our family dynamics are in large a part our responsibility and the way we govern is determined by how we face it. Many of us settle in the regrets of the last issue we deal with, odd right? Stagnantly we fold and force our life to fold with us. The issue is we cause that same behavior in our offspring, our children, and we have a problem seeing where we went wrong. It's never too late to make small changes in our children even when they've become adults. We just must be dedicated to doing so. Mahatma Ghandi said we should be the change we want to see in the world. We must take that seriously with our children, as they will be the most influential in being the change, we'd like to see in our world around us.

Change our thinking process, grow our lives in the simplest ways and be great at it. Our children are constantly looking at us for what they need, guidance to find which way life should take them. It's not until we allow the world of others make an impact that what we say might not to matter. Let your voice be the first voice heard as your children will need it. Let your phrases that impact life be those phrases used by your children because if you don't allow them to use yours, they will develop them by someone else's thinking.

The fabric of the society that surrounds your children forever lies in your hands. Make you count to your children.

May the peace of today be in your hands, may the peace in this moment guide the peace of the next moment for you and may you know your purpose. May your children's love for life come from yours and may your unpleasant habit become no more through your children's process of living. May your today be great or bring about greatness for your tomorrow.

I share love with you in this moment.

From my heart to yours,

Love,

The happy Bug

_____
_____
_____
_____
_____
_____
_____
_____
_____
_____
_____
_____
_____
_____
_____
_____
_____
_____
_____
_____
_____
_____
_____
_____
_____
_____

These pages are extending you the opportunity to write any thoughts that came to you during the process of reading this book. We are all writers whether we write like others or not. My hopes are for you to be free and write from your inner peace. I hope this brings you joy and freedom.
From my heart to yours,

Love,

The happy Bug

News Flash For all Readers

Our lives are made up of the experiences that we partake in but most importantly the experiences of those we surround ourselves with each day. It's unfortunate that nothing becomes an experience until we have learned from them. The goals, dreams and changes that will impact our lives, and the lives of our children, are as a result of what we create. The fact that we choose to make the bulk of our changes due to the thoughts of others - places us in a compromising position and can potentially become the driving focus of change for us as parents the leaders and our children who we've formed as the followers.

Too often as people we tend to believe that the way we see things is by right the correct way, and unfortunately when we are raising children we tend to forget that at some point we felt that our parents made some mistakes in raising us, otherwise we would never have felt to change to be different.

The issues with many parents is that everyone wants to be in control, because the child is thought to belong to one parent rather than the other. Unfortunately, Men a woman holds the right to be Parents because it's the law of nature, she's maternal. The state just followed that law is all so don't take it personal.

As people we must sit and think back on all the things that has happened around us and focus on them in a way that makes sense. I took a training class to learn how to

dissect people, which in turn would help me to better deal with people in my line of work. At that time, I was a Customer Service Specialist and indeed I loved what I did, however at that time I was very intolerable of stupidity and unfortunately people are just always going to be who they are. During the process of learning I've found what I was taught to be true.

70% of people are **reactors**;
they deal with and treat people
based on how they are
dealt with and treated
20% of people will always be
kind no matter what you do and
10% of people you **can't help**.

Each opportunity in our lives will create a new 100%, if we change a simple thought in our minds, we will be conscience of the way we deal with people and situations. It doesn't matter if we're dealing with baby mama or baby daddy, we are all still people and the breakdown explained earlier still applies. We must stop separating the people in our lives from the people outside of our lives, simply because we should not set expectations of others, we'd rather not have set upon us.

It seems far too evident that as people we put out things we'd rather not have to deal with.

It's a really bad situation that too many good men are falling to the wayside of discontent and dishonor and blatant disrespect. Moreover, it's sad that too many men of melanin feel targeted by the societies that surrounds them and their lives, and that too often the good men fall in the hand of not so good women and leaves a sour taste in their mouths.

I find it to be true that too many women of Melanin say that they need a man and when they get one they abuse him and disrespect him and diseasely treats him and dishonors him. I ask many woman why they feel the way they do and too often they say "Black Men" I like to call them "Men of Melanin" treats us like shit and don't respect us, meanwhile they seem to look for women of other ethnicities and treat them like queen then want us to deal with the shit they refuse to ask of other women of other ethnicities to do the same and ask us to take all their mishaps.

My opinion and we can argue a million times, is that so many men of melanin are trying to escape the Mother they were unable to protect from their father who hurt her but then I can be wrong. I hope the point was received that none of these things matter if were not willing to make simple changes.

The News Flash

The point is there can be fingers to point on both sides and it changes nothing, bills are still pressing; children are constantly being forced to choose sides and nothing is being accomplished. Could it be viewed the same if a woman applied this logic to her, if the roles were switched how many women would conquer that this is true for us to.

My goals are to connect the dots find the common ground and send the message that woman having fallen to the wayside of their society as well. Both men and woman have bad taste in their mouths about each other, unable to say if this affect causations or other races in these regards, we do know it is highly amongst us as people of melanin. I have a Caucasian friend who use to date "Black Men" men of Melanin and said behind closed doors she was treated like shit. When can we stop it, what can we do and how can we do it?

Let life happens; no matter who doesn't agree, no enemy matters if there's no enemy inside to unleash itself.

There is an African proverb that reads: "**When there is no enemy within, the enemy outside** can do you **no** harm."

Love you like I always will,
from my heart to yours

Love,
The happyBug

The happy Bug

Child Support

Child Support means- court-ordered payments, typically made by a noncustodial divorced parent, to support one's minor child or children. **Child Support** Uses. Parents may use **child support** to **cover** a broad array of expenses associated with the **child**. These include educational, health care and housing expenses, as well as family utility bills, mortgage payments, travel expenses, clothing and food. The purpose of child support is to protect the child from the economic impact of divorce or separation. Therefore, child support should be used for both the basic necessities of the child, such as food, shelter, childcare, and **education**, as well as the additional things that the child enjoyed during the marriage. However, **child** visitation **rights** are not based on whether a **father** pays **child support** or not. If a **father** has not legally lost his **child** visitation **rights**, he can seek court-ordered visitation. In some cases, unrelated to **child support**, a **father** can lose **child** visitation and **child** custody.

- Google

These were all sited because these are the issues that have been shared as being the problem for non- custodial parents. They never really know what a person does with the financial support they send for their children. I was deeply taken aback when I read the line about what Child Support is; women don't realize that these child support proceedings are based on a married couple and the children having to deal with the separation and less the financial disconnect. This means that as a unwed mothers we assume the responsibility of taking care of our children alone. The reason is because one ever entered into a contract or promise to aide you in taking care of your children. It is assumed that support should only be granted to a mother whose womb has been wed, no shade intended.

Awareness is how we jumpstart change, in order to create something magical we must get started on it. We'll plan our destination for a million years but until the journey has begun the destination sits dormant and unreached, and the solution goes unattained. There has been such an overwhelming unresponsive approach to child support and the issues of child support enforcement. Child support for whatever reason has such a negative undertone. In my opinion, child support is not remotely as bad as people think about it, it's the enforcement that people really have a problem with. It's the feel of being out of control of the situation – overstandably because studies show that people don't like to be told what they need to do, they rather be in charge their affairs. The issue with this understanding is simply that children, like people and things, need maintenance. Most people take baths each day, we stop by the gas station to put gas in the cars we drive, we buy new clothes and shoes. Whether we've grown accustomed to having new things or were in need of a garment for a certain occasion, it bears a necessity. Children are much the same and at times require more maintenance than self, because it's a battle of the mind, body and soul. Our children are the platform in which the foundation can be laid and formed.

 The way we think in the face of rearing them will be very instrumental in their outcome. It's bad enough that when we send our children to school each day, we find ourselves reparenting them all over again, having to replaster the foundation for proper direction and even then, it's not enough. Men and women need to realize how much of themselves they need to give to their children in order for them to be proper. Though at times no matter how much you sow into them you still might be one off based on how they soak in the environment around them. No matter if you raise your children Rich or Poor the bad influences are very eminent to their growth or their failure. As parents we must seek a common goal or the medium in which children will be cared for. More men need to step up to being better and more mothers need to get a bigger fork and eat up. Stop telling these men you don't need them. Our civilization is at stake if we don't step up and make the difference, instead of sitting around waiting for other people to do so.

I conducted a set of interviews with both men and women. In this dedicated article the responses will be shared. Please be aware they are heart felt. The goal of this article is to show the commonality between those who were reached, set as a platform for more people to get together and become the change that's needed, and to find where the change is needed most. I'll Thank you in advance for your consideration of this information.

Child support is merely a term. Although it is court ordered to establish financial support for custodial parents raising children, it's certainly the enforcement that's' really detested.

Despite what it seems to be when someone is giving you money rather by force or by free will, it's important to show them how their money is being spent. Don't take a person's money and don't use for the betterment of the child or children it's meant to support. No one wants to see their children whom they pay child support for, with raggedy or dingy clothes, shoes with holes in them or worse nothing decent to go anywhere with. Since, we have a right to ration how we will spend out money, we still get to ration out how we will spend our money as the mother or custodial parent, we still have that choice. It's so often we don't realize how simple things can create gigantic issues, usually because most people think about themselves and their feelings. Not that these situations are always true, or always apply there's some truth in the matter.

The Opinions of those interviewed are in their own words

Questions

1. Do you think child Support is necessary?
Abraham(male): Yes, because the child needs financial assistance and the mother needs the help so that she can spend more time with child.
Wonderous (female): Said no, because as a mother you assume the responsibility to take care of them no matter what happens.
Shatory (female): Yes, because without it some people would help with anything. It helps to get them what they need.
Crystal (female): No
William: "Hell Yeah, for the parents aren't doing shit"
Terrance (Male): In some cases, yes. In my case no I take care of my children and because I just had a new baby my children mom says she's trying to beat my current girlfriend to the punch assuming our relationship won't work. I take care of my children.
Julian (male): No, I took good care of my children
Wayne (male): Yes
Patrick(male): Yes
Tavares (male): Yes for people who don't take care of their children
Tony (male): Yes, some people need to be made to do for their children.

2. Are you now or were you the Custodial or Non-Custodial Parent?

Abraham: Custodial for 2 children and until 3 months ago non-custodial for 1 of my children

Do you think a non-custodial parent should go to jail because they don't pay Child Support?

Wonderous: Custodial

Shatory: Custodial

Crystal: Custodial

William: Custodial and non-custodial

Terrance: My children live 3-day week with me and 4 with their mother, I consider myself Custodial/Non-Custodial

Julian: Non-Custodial

Patrick: Non-custodial

Wayne: Non-custodial

Tavares: Was non-custodial now I am custodial I have sole custodial now.

3. How does child support raise children?

Abraham: It doesn't, what it does help free up some time for the custodial parent, so they don't have to pick up a second job taking the time they need to be there for the children.

Wonderous: It helps the custodial parent get what's necessary for the children, but it doesn't really raise them.

Shatory: It takes away the stress, even though more could be used in many different ways.

Crystal: child support financially helps to provide the basic necessities possible by help celebrating, birthday, taking trips taking care of those things that are rarely accounted for that children need.

William: Child support raising the child depends on how the custodial parent spend the money.

Terrance: For non-custodial parents it helps them pay bills when the bills are due.

Julian: No, if the child is not getting it.

Tavares: Feed them, houses them and buys school supplies.

4. Do you think it is necessary for a non-custodial parent to go to jail for not paying child support?

Abraham: Yes, only because if they are doing for the child, that means they are running from their responsibility.

Wonderous: No, it's not the answer if they still can't provide if they are in jail.

Shatory: No, but I understand why it's enforced.

Crystal: No, because going to jail doesn't help, while there in jail the custodial parent is still without financial support.

William: Hell, yeah if you let it build up enough that you have to go to jail them that means you are assuming your responsibility.

Terrance: No, because you can't force feed people to do anything.

Julian: No
Patrick: No
Wayne: No
Tavares: Some guys should

5. What would your advice be to man not paying child support?

Abraham: Put money in an account and keep record, give the custodial parent access that way you'll have record of what is being spent from the child support account.

Wonderous: You should take your responsibilities serious; children are an experience unless you're not willing to be in their lives.

Shatory: Your child is suffering because you don't see the needs that he or she is faced with. You can't possibly think about the welfare of your children when you're eating.

Crystal: If you can't do anything financially be present because that's more important than money.

William: Pay your child support or it will continue to go up, no excuses payment plans are available.

Terrance: If you want your children to succeed your child support should be paid.

Julian: Get a job - you got to take care of the baby.

Patrick: Try find the connections with your child.

Tavares: Just pay something even if you don't have it all. I think some guys just don't love their children which is why so many of them don't want to pay.

6. What is your advice to a woman who's not getting child support on how to handle the drought of the absent parent?

Abraham: Plan for the absent parent. If the absent parent is always late paying child support don't plan to pay your bills with that money.

Wonderous: Just do what has to be done. Let go of the leverage, if the man is helping, he's showing effort let go of spite you don't have to be in control keep him out of the system.

Shatory: Still be the best Mother you can be.

Crystal: Meditate, pray, learn to be appreciative of what you do have and be dedicated to your children.

7. How much child support do you receive?

Abraham: None

Wonderous: He was ordered to pay $660.00 through divorce decree, Dad paid 160/week faithfully which totaled $640.00 and he even paid extra if the children needed it and still helps the children who are now adults. Funny because he didn't think it was necessary to travel the children so if I needed extra for that I was on my own, but I respected that because he didn't feel it was necessary, we shared 4 children.

Shatory: The order was for $529 he pays 488.00 which is $122/Weekly

Crystal: My sons dad took literally took care of all his needs and even provide me financial support when I was in need. He would even buy grocery for my house when I couldn't, he often made me feel like I wasn't doing enough, because he left me with nothing to worry about.

William: Not on child support, I pay $150.00 weekly and more if needed.

8. Who does not receiving child support effect? Mom or Child

Abraham: The child and he custodial parent.

Shatory:

Crystal: for my household if the children and the custodial parent because if there is no other income coming in it affects the children as well as the custodial parent.

William: Seems like the mom because she always asks for more than she needs

Patrick: Child

Wayne: Mom if she doesn't do right with the money

Tavares: It affects the children if they don't have what he or she needs

9. Do you pay child support?

Abraham: Yes; Wonderous: No; Shatory: No; Crystal: No; William: Yes; Terrance: No; Patrick: No; Wayne: No; Tavares: Yes

10. How much do you pay? How often?

Abraham: $300.00/Month at times 1 ½ months depending on how much I had at the time. (I now have all my children in my custody)

Wonderous: Received $640/month

William: $600/monthly

Julian: $900/Month Owe 17K Backpay as long as I'm working

Wayne: $800.00

Tavares: $600/month

11. How does paying child support effect your financial situation?

Abraham: If I had extra; I sent extra, at times I went without and my children that lives with me went without too. There were times I didn't eat.

Wayne: It often puts me in a bind, I have a couple families to care for not just the baby they're taking so much money for especially when I take care of him anyway.

Tavares: Left me dead broke, and homeless they're taking all my income.

12. Who do you think it helps when you pay child support? The child or the Mom?

Abraham: It helps them both, because when I paid it took the weigh off her so that the mom could spend more time with my son not having to worry about money.

Wonderous: Mom. It helps with whatever needs to be taken care of at the moment.

Crystal: Both

William: Mom

Terrance: Child even if the cash pays for the lights

Patrick: Mom

Wayne: Mom

Tavares: Mom, depending on how she spends that money because all parents aren't the same.

13: Do you think child support cover enough of your child's bare necessities?

Abraham: Absolutely not. I am a person who believes to expect the unexpected. Like in case a parent has a break down with he car who's going to pay for it, child needs to get where he or she's going.

Wonderous: No

Shatory: No

Crystal: No. Because the amount that's stated a non-custodial should pay is not enough. Every little bit helps but doesn't make it enough.

William: Yes

Terrance: No. If custody is split it should be enough

Patrick: yes

Wayne: Yes

Tavares: No.

14. How much of yourself can you dedicate to your child if you can't afford to pay?

Abraham: All my time away from work

Crystal: 365/24/7. I said you can't possibly spend that time with your children. She said I work for my children, because theirs many days I don't feel like getting up

Terrance: A lot; Wayne: 12 Hours; Patrick: All my extra time

15. How important is time?

Abraham: Right now, time is not important, right now I'm so focus on surviving I don't have that luxury to worry about time.

Wonderous: Very, it's everything, it's more than money

Shatory: 100%

Crystal: Very because we give them will mold them into the adults they will become, and it creates memories.

William: Time is more important than anything. Fathers need to raise their children because my mom had the block raising me.

Terrance: Very

Patrick: Very important, almost more than money

Tavares: Time is valued more than money

16. How can the pressures of child support be solved in your opinion?

Abraham: They need to focus on everything, evaluations need to take place; let go of the bias against the non-custodial parent.

Wonderous: No one really has the answer.

Crystal: I think if the Fathers felt they had more control it'll be better. Like allotting how the money is spent; it'll take down so of the issues of child support.

William: Put more focus on the needs of the children rather than money, build programs for parents who can't be of financial assistance.

Wayne: Give equal rights

Patrick: Give equal rights.

Last but certainly not least.

17. By your definition what are bare necessities?

Abraham: Food, Rent, Lights, Gas for the car, Clothes but not monthly.

Wonderous: Food, clothing, Medical, Shelter, Extracurricular activities because it gives them an outlet. Travelling creates exposure, transportation, field trips and phone.

Shatory: Rent, Lights, Water, Food, Phone, Gas, Personal items, hair and entertainment.

Crystal: Food, Shelter, Clothing, Medical, transportations.

Williams: Shoes, seasonal clothing (from New York), food, shelter, supplies.

Terrance: Shelter, Food, entertainment, Light, Transportation, Gad and Water

Julian: Shelter, Food and Clothes.

Patrick: Shelter, Food and Clothes,

Wayne: Shelter, Food and clothes

Tavares: Food, Shelter, clothes, Transportation

Wonderous: The child most. It also effects the child If the custodial parent is not stable and that creates stress.

There are some great dedicated Fathers and Mothers, the stigmas have been the epitome of parental progress showing itself as failure and the question is how to we stop it. Our first goal would be for our parents to learn how to value each other and possibly that'll create us able to give the children all they need un-egotist. Our journey is so far from reached but in order to reach our goal we must start the process. May this article reach you in your peaceful place.

From My heart to yours,

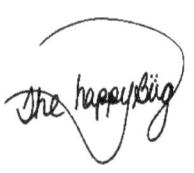

Qualities of a Good Mother

A mother's qualities are so powerful they often are directive,
depending upon her passion she is likely truly respected.
She's also the protector, and in her heart she's pure,
although she has a hard time being corrected, because she's
really sure.
Her greatest skill is that she's the leader and her power make
her courageous,
her optimism makes her dedicated and her willingness
maker her ability to love and be caring.
Her development has created loyalty and at times, although
it's not easy to accept her honesty
is always direct because her goals is to protect.
Her precision is out of the ordinary it makes her ways seem
dramatic;
the moment she spiritually connected gave her all her
strength.
Her strong-minded disposition makes her the
backbone of her family the matriarch of her name,
and it's unfortunate that once she has gone on to
glory her family won't be the same.
At times she seems perturbed because she wants
what's best for her family, she at times lives in fear,
and the fact that everyone flocks to her
leadership makes her truly special

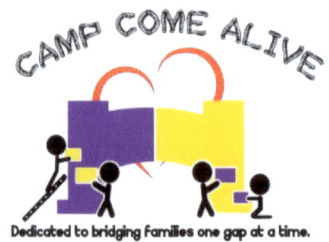

Dedicated to bridging families one gap at a time.

Our Mission
Camp Come Alive Inc.

Camp Come Alive Inc. is a fundraising company offering advocate services to non-custodial parents paying child support rather current or in arrears. Although our major goal is to reach as many non-custodial parents, we also provide aid to custodial parents who should be receiving child support income as well. We provide our members with one-on-one assistance throughout the fundraising process. Our teams consist of non-custodial parents, including those who are incarcerated. Our target audience will be those residing in low income areas of Broward, Dade, and Palm Beach Counties, but not limited to only those who resides in those areas.

Camp Come Alive is dedicated to helping bridge the gap wedged between families due to financial hardships, child support, and neglect which is an unpleasant reality for all parties involved. The purpose of our organization is to restructure the family unit in a positive way through family involved activities, fundraising, family counseling and personal skill building workshops. As an organization, we also take old furniture and refurbish the upholstery with inspirational poetry, slogans, and personalized messages.

We have created a sales force to distribute and market T-shirts, pillows, blankets and other household items with positive messages. Our fundraising efforts include selling those T-shirts, refurbishing the furniture, accepting monetary donations and collecting cans for recycling. We also host fundraisers to help garner support and raise revenue for those in the community with child support deficits.
Our goal is to rebuild self-worth!

A strong sense of self-worth helps parents become better mentors and role models to their children, providing real-world coping strategies with everyday struggles. We also offer parenting skill set classes and involvement sessions to help bring struggling families together.

Our value reflects Growth, Unity, Integrity, Persistence, and Hard work!
Camp Come Alive Inc. aims to strengthen the community and the heart. We will without failure honor that philosophy with our concrete values. We will remain committed to meeting each participant's needs and keeping them connected during the process.
Camp Come Alive Inc. Dedicated to bridging families one gap at a time.

Behind on Payments?
Have you been Purged?

NEED HELP
Paying Child Support?
WE ARE NOT A REFERRAL SERVICE

GIVE US A CALL
954.709.5259
Our Services Are FREE!

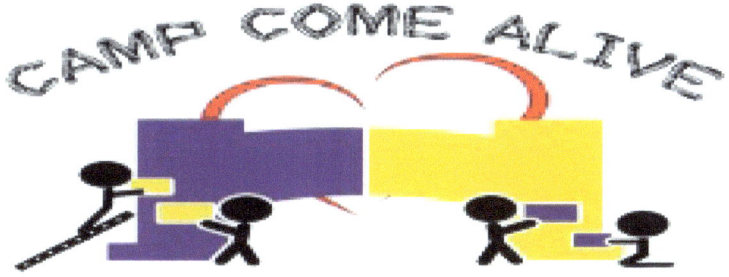

CAMP COME ALIVE

Dedicated to bridging families; one gap at a time.

"Let Us Be Your Advocate"

Contact Information

Campcomealive@yahoo.com

Facebook/campcomealive

Instagram.com/campcomealive

www.campcomealive.org

It always seems impossible until it's done
- Nelson Mandela

Child Abuse

The worst kind of child abuse is what can't be seen, children bruised inside by the broken fiend. Addicted to so much hurt, sadly they are passing along the pain after being damaged first.

People abuse children's spirits each day, no arrests take place, brutally murdering true concepts of life no guided pace. Walking around with blinders on around the brain, at times not even as much guidance than the horse, no destination driven to stay on course. Who's parenting the parents no real way to truly do it, having babies bitterly waiting on a situation to prove it. So, who's right? One parent situation one sided fights. No opposites to make a difference, no true second chances. Parents before them destroyed their dreams so there goes another generation, blatantly having disgraced another situation - no one saving faces.

It's unfortunate that too often people don't really get to know each other before they begin making babies, now people are throwing blows saying their partner is shady - but you didn't even really get to know them before you actually find yourself now having to share a baby. Another statistic let's be realistic.

Knowing people's past making decisions because of it without judging them for it, so be real - some people have been through too much to heal. Too many issues to be of any true value to another life, some men aren't built to be husbands and some women aren't built to be wives. Perfect chance to break the cycle, no reason to cry over broken promises or expectations some people can't live up to, no need to further break a person down having to prove to you.

Sometimes people have been through so much they can only pass the suffering on their children; heaving blisters of experienced pain, thrown out to the wolves it's all the same. Too many people avoiding change, easier to pass the blame.

Bitter bitten people raise bitter bitten children. One dream killed by deadened visions. Families feel like they are followed by family curses, and what's worse is, people are too broken to make a solid effort to change it, too protected against others scrutiny to make light of it. What they think to be self-protection, becomes the destruction of another generation.

No holding their hands, no deliverance no chance.

This chart breaks down how your monetary support compares to your children's living situation?

The government says on average it costs $900.00/Month to properly raise one child, so to be fair they split the cost down the middle. That is calculated to be $450.00/parent, which is why some people pay $450.00 as a base. The average child support order being paid is only $275.00/Month.

The totals below are the values based on $450.00 if each parent is equally paying the cost per the government order divided into 7 bills. These numbers are based on the author's household.

Bill Type	Cost	Applied Child Support	Balance Owed
Rent	1,100.00	64.28	1,035.72
Lights	240.00	64.28	175.72
Water	170	64.28	105.72
Phone	120	64.28	55.72
Food	730.00	64.28	665.72
Gas	320	64.28	255.72
Entertainment	150	64.28	85.72
Clothes/Shoes	80.00	Not enough child support to stretch Can be offset	
Co-Pays	60.00	Not enough child support to stretch	
Field Trips	35.00	Not enough child support to stretch Can be Offset	
Car Note	482.00	Not enough child support to stretch	
Car Insurance	280.00	Not enough child support to stretch	
Corner Store	30.00 Wkly	Not enough child support to stretch	
First day of School	Can't be paid for	Invaluable	
GRAND TOTAL	$3,797.00	$450.00	$3,347.00

CHILD SUPPORT

Child support only supports the order of financial tension; sit back and listen,
Take it all in; grab yourself a piece of paper and a pen.
If Child support is all you have to give.
Let's break it down, then tell me how dollars bills are worth your child's smile.
According to the government it takes **$900.00**/month to properly raise one child, Sounds kind of wild? I know take out your pen divide **$900.00** by your number of bills, subtract that amount from a household that was already top heavy, and tell me would you like to be left begging?
That home was already struggling before you helped add another leg,
and you don't want to contribute to how the entire household gets fed?

That's kind of stupid!

Now you don't want to help pay for a situation you were once partly using;
and had no problem once abusing.
Your responsibility is not over because she closed her legs,
And you don't need to feel like a man by having her beg
You knew it would be harder once another child was added to an already stressed out condition,
now you want to go on no longer being attentive?
Was it your jealousy wanting what he had so you felt to plant your seed?
now you realize that you are no better than he?

Blame can be toggled between both parties;
so let's give you some ease, it doesn't always cost money to please.
Children's pleasures are simple and more delicate whatever you're able to put in,
like the valuable daddy's play to make their daughters comfortable in their skin.
But go on I'll wait; you like to drag your feet sending in those child support payments late.
You're only obligated to pay half and in some cases not even,
so, take your 450 divide it by 7 bills that gives you $65.00 dollars

to each bill rounded to nearest dollar,

Ask yourself is that enough money for you to live?
Child support doesn't factor in toiletries or under clothes, for girls'
pads and pantyhose, for young men haircuts or cologne, should I go
on?
When children get sick all the medicine that Medicaid doesn't cover,
becomes a daunting task for a mother.
Get out of your own way you have yet to factor in birthdays and
vacays
and forget about simple gifts,
or even the toys your children play with?

Seems quite simple?

What about schools supplies that can't possibly be considered;
and you wonder what's the cause of a woman being bitter.
You're not factoring in enough you're simply just scraping across the
surface;
you don't even consider the role you play of making a not so great
situation feel perfect.

_____
_____
_____
_____
_____
_____
_____
_____
_____
_____
_____
_____
_____
_____
_____
_____
_____
_____
_____
_____
_____
_____
_____
_____
_____
_____
_____

These pages are extending you the opportunity to write any thoughts that came to you during the process of reading this book. We are all writers whether we write like others or not. My hopes are for you to be free and write from your inner peace. I hope this brings you joy and freedom.

From my heart to yours,

Love, *The happy Bug*

The happy Bug

Be patient and tough and someday this pain will be useful to you
- Ovid

EXTENDED FAMILIES

Men don't often really consider, what they are doing to the mother of their children. When they choose to go out with all these women; baring new seeds; thinking only from their perspectives. Not realizing all the problems, they are gaining during the process of the other problems that are being neglected, caring less about all involved being affected.

Building walls around the issues, telling self-that's what he wished to- just to keep from looking stupid, knowing that your reasons makes no sense and that you're just passing out excuses.

Broken children don't usually have a voice to speak, assuming that all the problems they've watched their mother succumb to has rendered her weak. This is what has happened to our cultured brothers, unable to be loyal to a cultured woman because he had to sit back and watch while his father walked over his mother. Too afraid to pay patronage to his mother's pain, when he too becomes the same type of man who put the hurt upon his mother's face. Self-hate is no escape; a woman is still a woman no matter the skin upon her face. You see the tears we drink in front of our daughters teaches them resentment, because at the time they are the only ones we can cry to who won't judge Mother - for her struggles, and the only souls we can trust that we know won't betray us. Growing up only to become the same person through empathy they protected, all because the Father was too self-indulgent to realize all the issues, he left unattended, all the feelings he left unprotected, and the rules to the game he so blatantly disrespected.

Men and women full of deceptive thinking, belittling the current situation for other things. Like, just the moment, only later to realize that what you fight to have you really didn't want it. Sisters and brothers falling through the cracks of being unloved, relationships never developed, and if daddy ever became unashamed of his past has to now embellish. There's really no truth in the matter, now the adult who was once a broken child is asking for these answers. Never to get an understanding, why the parents couldn't keep it together long enough for him or her not to grow up feeling abandoned. Once again leaving this person feelings shattered, because selfish reasons most commonly don't have solid answers. Now here comes the fabrication him saying he never made any outside babies, now the mother who was once sure is no longer sure and you can't see that as shady?
The betrayed woman's lying to herself telling herself she's been vindicated, thinking that he chose her in the situation when the ingredients in the pudding says he was never dedicated. He just too became too ashamed, so he made her feel she was the choice, maybe having no strength of a man because he never really had HIS voice.
Hats off to the fathers who have always claimed their children unaffected by his woman's feelings; doesn't change the fact that, that woman has gone unprotected – now the fate of your children's relationships is in the hand of their mother's if they have yet to accept it.

Not every woman becomes strong enough to understand, but by then it doesn't make a difference, she stayed in the situation right down to the minute that it was really finished. Women often settle in the shame, being the woman who the man she loved so dishonorably betrayed. Everyone is trying now to keep it a secret; because the other woman had the baby after he begged her not to keep it. The baby has grown up starts calling the man daddy, the first woman doesn't want people to know she wasn't the only woman keeping her man happy. Can you blame the child for being free, appreciating every bit of the good the father had come to be, love disables what hate allows one to see? By now she may truly get it, it was hard for you to walk away, now all the pain she endured too deeply scared her and she may never be able to escape.

So, Man, where lies your fate?

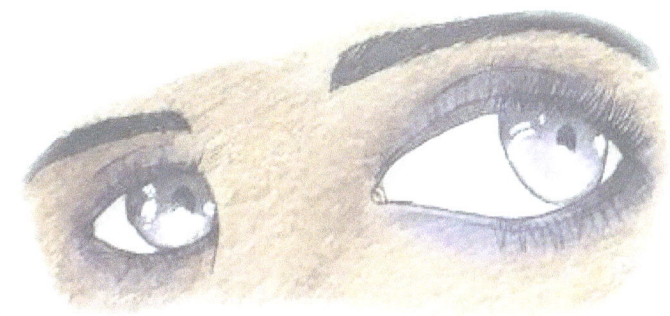

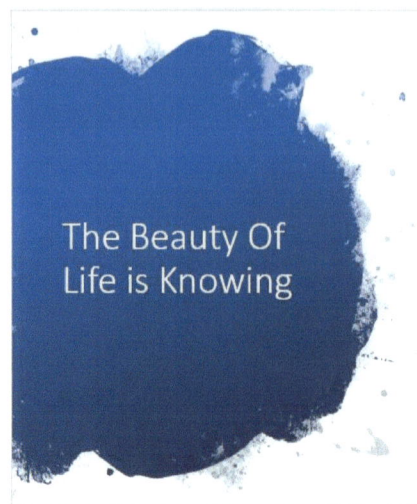

The Beauty Of Life is Knowing

- Yesterday is history
- Tomorrows a Mystery
- Today is a Gift That's Why It's called
- The **Present**

\-   **Author Unknown**

Life in itself is a teacher and you are in a state of constant learning
- Bruce Lee

The Story Behind It Is What It Is

When parents are hurt it often leaves their children in the middle, living up to the apologies for their parents' never assumed or never accepted mistakes. *It Is What It Is* is a piece written as an unapologetic apology to my sisters for my expressions about their ema. My feelings were often stemmed from a place of hurt or fear and misinterpreted as anger and/or malicious behavior, when in fact it was often just a cry for help. It was commonly thought that I had ill intensions and hate for my Aba's first wife when in truth I never did.

I come from a plural family. For many years I thought that as long as my siblings and I shared Aba, we were all sisters and brothers which made us the same. I learned very abruptly that was not true; my siblings and I were very different and only ½ of our blood was the same because we have different ema's. Their Ema had the heart of my sisters, and for so long I was unable to make sense of that. I had to deal with whatever decision she made, right wrong or indifferent. If I wanted to spend the night with them or even invite them to bathe in my living quarters, their ema had the upper hand and her decision was always final. So, when I would lash out, often it was simply me trying to express that I felt there were no differences between myself and my sisters. In retrospect I realize the difference was major because the fact remained that she was their ema and I wasn't her daughter.

My Aba and Ema raised me to believe that my siblings and I were all one, but there was a disconnect with the family dynamics. Not everyone felt safe in dealing with the situation for reasons maybe only they would overstand. I believe the pain that my sisters' Ema suffered during the process of the transition from her normal life made her uncomfortable as she was dealing with a situation she never imagined. She was faced with having to accept her husband's open infidelities. Many lives were altered during this process and the fact that I was bred to overstand that this was my life's reality, I often could not accept what made her feel she had the right to be upset. Life changed so rapidly that I found it easier to live by only what I thought was truth rather than that what had been fed to me to believe.

I wholeheartedly believe in speaking what my heart feels is truth. Unfortunately, it is not always well received. *It Is What It Is* is a deep dedication to those who were once pained by the reality of our life's perfect truths.

It Is What It Is

Sorry for your Mother's pain, two women different interest found one thing the same.
I'll tell you something that might set her ahead, no one thinks that she's stupid just gainsaid.
No one thinks that she's crazy just in the state of denial,
it just doesn't make sense that you've hurt all this while.
When a person has moved on to another place you can't continue to hold to their misfed truths,
you have to forgive let's move ahead,
stop walking the path of the living dead,
because the misery you feel only you can truly feel; only you can think your thoughts,
and only you can help you heal.
                                        Because,
When a woman can't see her faults and that man can't see his, you have got to come to grips with it,

It Is What It Is

Share an embracing arm with this unchangeable tribe,
We love you because he Loved you this is Why.
You're blaming children born just like yours,
Asked your children to hate their blood because you're sore.
We all know how easy it is to fall in the state of disbelief,
When you know the truth to the reason you can't sleep.
It's easy to deal when you think no one else knows,
When you don't have to deal with all the woes,
or even have to be ashamed,
When people are pointing fingers at you with blame. But,
Mistreated years won't be forgotten like all your pain never left at sudden.
There's a broken heart almost to go insane –
thinking back on the day my mother almost died when I was 5,
she would've died with me thinking that she didn't love me
because of all the things you allowed yourself to do to me.

Later to realize she didn't know,
and when I come to learn she really loved me I was able to grow.
Now you want to be completely forgiven when you never forgave,
it's like asking God to protect a soul he never saved.
Because,
When a woman can't see her faults and that man can't see his, you
have got to come to grips with it,
It Is What It Is.

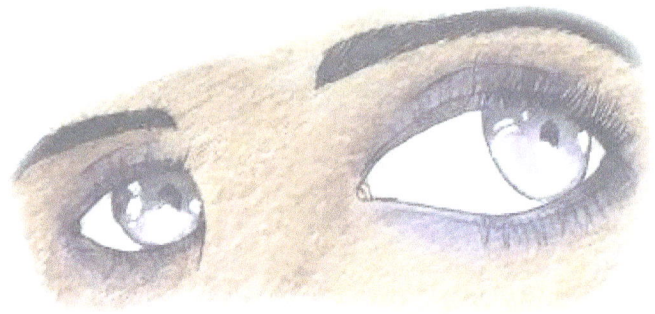

I Forgave

I forgave for the sake of forgiveness,
I forgave before I knew it would come to this
I forgave you a long time ago,
I forgave even for answers I did not know.
I forgave all the hurt and pain,
I forgave even though all the prayers seemed in vain.
I forgave first because of you
I forgave before Yahweh did what He had to do.
I forgave for all the tears I'd cry
I forgave you without knowing why
I forgave you, Ema and Aba said I had to
I forgave and gained love for you
Before I could enter heavens gates, I had to forgive you
now I can stand with my head held tall now I'm at liberty
I didn't learn to forgive you for you, I forgave you for me.

It's A Woman

Her pussy has a heartbeat, flutters like butterflies in the stomach when you speak. Like the heart flutters with an overflow of blood when you're near, she drips saturated heavily when she thinks of your stare. That desire that SHE possess knowing that you want her, she goes off the chemistry that your parts share when energy made transfers. Two different things sharing the same experience the only thing you can do is respect the moment and go into the thought of the very last enjoyment. Potent to its wishes, craving for your kisses. Starving with this strong inclination, love deep enough to exhibit so much patience. She finds herself at work squirming in her seat, crossed legs and clinched feet. At that moment living in the experience, having to clear her throat when she has flashbacks of certain periods - reminiscing over how she didn't know what was next to be expected, and no matter how much she tries to release the memory her mind, her body or spirit wouldn't allow her to let it become disconnected.

Now she sits almost dormant in my fears, gitters and tears. Nervous and unassured, now loving you doesn't make her feel secured. Slightly a bit scared wondering if the two of you were even sharing, in the moment and if you had a bit of what she considered caring. Hearing the loud of silence in her thoughts that maybe you'd tell me to get out of my feelings, body feeling hot yet going through these chilling's. She waited - shared her body with you and you faked it, now she's feeling a little broken - allowed to many words to be unspoken. Unthought thinking, now she's shrinking - feeling a bit like wishful thinking.
You can't take all a person has and give them only a piece of what you have to offer and don't expect that they will behave the way you think they should, sharing food with their minds and laying wood. Having passed too many years, sharing bodily fluids, and listening ears. Going out of the way to one sided injunctions, having changed her daily functions. Compromising making little changes, now you're acting like you're brainless.

That's when she snaps, called you and you don't call back. Texting with no reply, too ashamed to cry. So, she goes into my safe place - little questions in her head; like was it just a test? was it an experience for us both or was it just like sex? All the same, making love to her brain.

Now you're acting like you don't get it, you shared each other as confidants you betrayed her - you should've known she wasn't the perfect person to just lay with. She honors her person, careful with most people but because of where you come from it was you, she trusted. Only for you to be like all those from whom she shied away, realized you only wanted to be her fiend, addicted to the thought of the comfort you pretended to bring. The tables begin to serve a different meal - she had an epiphany, wake HER up from her deepest sleep. Un-fooled, unapologetic, unwavering, now unaffected, trusted you no protection, shared all her love and affection - never shared herself with anyone else. A woman deserves to be respected honored not neglected or mistreated, feeling like she's been pushed to the limits of being defeated, no need to repeat it. Women are persons not possessions, you'll find when you need her the most she'll be less to be needed, she use to need it all from you now she needs all of none of it.

_____
_____
_____
_____
_____
_____
_____
_____
_____
_____
_____
_____
_____
_____
_____
_____
_____
_____
_____
_____
_____
_____
_____
_____
_____
_____
_____
_____

These pages are extending you the opportunity to write any thoughts that came to you during the process of reading this book. We are all writers whether we write like others or not. My hopes are for you to be free and write from your inner peace. I hope this brings you joy and freedom.
From my heart to yours,

Love,

The happy Bug

The happy Bug

Real Nigga Shit

The first comes too often the rent is due,
You received your last paycheck to cover a few.

Lights

Water

Phone

Food

Insurance

Car Loan.

Next week all your bills will soon become overdue and the money you received on your paycheck will only cover you for Two, which 2 do you choose when you run out of cash? That's some
Real Nigga Shit for Your Ass.
Find yourself drawing around the line to protect the one you're with, sit back and take some more of this Real Nigga Shit.
You feel you're the wife of a very special man, you thought of him to be your very special friend, you begin looking around not knowing what to do, then you find out he's been cheating on you. Heart break we've all endure, relationships no longer secure, and believing in each other is no longer a factor in your life, because there is no more beauty in being his wife. Now he's denying the fact that he has been doing the do now that the light is shining on the truth, he's screaming out it's not his kid, when he should have never done what he did. The wife finds out and she goes kind of crazy, because the honesty to this mess looks rather hazy. So she begins asking questions like how did this all begin? Wondering how he came to the decision of betraying his only true friend. "I don't want that Bitch any more anyway" you sound really stupid did you not have anything else to say? You weren't saying all that shit when you were riding her ass, saying sweet things to make the moment last, now you're around here selling that girl false dreams, it's like giving a cashier a coupon that can't be redeemed. The other woman has found that she's been deceived so now she's upset, because she hadn't been hipped to this
Real Nigga Shit.

Then the table started to take different turn, the wife no longer looking for what her body yearned, he was taking her loving giving it away for free, the wife that she had been footing the fee. She learned that the hearts damaged can never be undone, she learned to bite the bullet of the smoking gun. Sometimes it not worth leaving your home, she learned to sing a different type of song, and the truth leaks out to that man, now he's acting like he doesn't understand, his mind goes to wondering can it really be true? That all the while he's been cheating on her she's been cheating on him too?

Oh you thought you were the only one getting a thrill, she was on her own agenda enjoying the field; no body to catch her you laying with another woman pussy on your dick, now you find out your girl got you back now she ain't shit. What about the woman you were fucking with? What makes her better than your girl if your bitch ain't shit? What you thought she pulled out some of those veteran moves? Putting that good pussy on that nigga because he ain't you? Or did you think he was hitting her pussy better than because your game must not have been tight because you've been cheating to? Now you want to know what she let the next man do, if she's holding on to him who's holding on to you?

Love is gone baby you're blinded by the past, that's some

Real Nigga Shit for Your Ass.

A Man is what he think about all day
- 	Emerson

Accepting What it means to be A Broken Woman

Womanhood is being able to say, that you withstood the test of having your most extreme heartbreak, back when you were the girl who loved the way you loved to look into your daddy's eyes, back when you knew what it meant to be a prize. When you were the girl who could believe her man even when your friends told you he was telling you lies, before you realize his truth was disguised. When you thought that you were able to cope with anything, that you were the absolute best, back before you were nothing like the rest. That you were the only woman in the world that he'd find so special and that no matter what you did for him he'd still find something that he could not find in you in her. That although you've blinded yourself from where he fell in flaws, that you didn't have to worry that behind your back that would be building walls; of distrust, because the man you thought loved you was just swimming in his lust. Now all the trust and love you'd developed is now just a wasted feeling, because you realized that this man you love was just going on in his dealings. So, when you're lying in your bed, sick to no end, like a little small girl who just lost her best friend. You don't want to cook or shower, and too ashamed to see anybody because you were so caught up in the mode of loving without any limitation, now you have to go back and revamp your personal invitation; to control all those angered deadly feelings, because you want to know the truth to this man and all his dealings. Like when you trusted his word that he needed to be alone, all those nights you thought he was chilling when you were left at home. Was he looking into her eyes with the look you so vividly remember; and so secretly adored, now it just like every other memory that you wish you could abort? Your conversation is tears, because you can see everything so clear, now you just don't want to revisit all those broken trusts and hurts.

You Betrayed Me with The Cheating

When I first met you it was everything I could imagine, I never worried about anyone before me and I could never fathom anyone would come after. Dancing in the ambiance of being your girl and when you married me; what satisfaction, that I was your wife - I had to do my duties and that in itself was the gift there would be no room for other distractions.

During the process of all the broken emotions and the self-repairing from all the deceit, at times I feel loss of what I ever loved you for because you made me feel I had to compete. Love should never hurt even during times when their will be pain, love is supposed to alleviate the impact of stress helping me become able to sustain.

Now I question my woman, which is my position, question my ability to provide you completion and that maybe I am not capable of completely carrying out my wifely mission. At the time I trusted you most you betrayed me no one could've ever told me that we'd be in this place, and that another woman would be threatening my personal place. I thought that all I'd been molded to be was a perfect fit for you, and that anything else quite like me would come too few. Yet, you seemed to have been looking for something different not perfect, and every woman would have the possibilities to be my worry. Nothing for myself, now the relationship I'd built would leave me nothingness. You want me to turn a blind eye to everything you could have protected me from, my heart has lost some of its rhythm it moves at times as if he doesn't really have a beat, and the tears I've choked from has really rendered me unable to speak.

I have forgiven you but at times some things you do remind me of when I trusted you most, so into protection I have to go to protect myself unlike I was able to do before.
When I lay down awaiting you to take over me; waiting for your embrace, reminds me of when I waited for you to return home when you had another woman caressing your face. Or your body, maybe your mind - those things I'd never know, because my eyes can only see what's physically present and you were behind someone else's door. Laying in someone else bed being neglectful of your own, you'd lie down in comfort in another woman's bed when you could have been laying down at home. Together we've made our babies, what an experience that would come to be, I'd waited to have a family with someone that was meant for only me. I've stood in the paint for love, but you didn't choose me first, when you hurt me you hurt me forever; most time people don't repair, from their hurt.

Just because you're not seeking it doesn't mean I don't need it. So, when I tell you I need more than you've given be careful with how I'm feeling. I know you love me I love you to; even though I forgave you doesn't change my perspective of ever being hurt, just like you say it doesn't mean that you chose her when you dealt with her and that you didn't put her first.

What Strikes the Writer in you?

These pages are extending you the opportunity to write any thoughts that came to you during the process of reading this book. We are all writers whether we write like others or not. My hopes are for you to be free and write from your inner peace. I hope this brings you joy and freedom.
From my heart to yours,

Love,
The happy Bug

The happy Bug

Man of Culture

If God is a woman? Who is Man? The protector of all he surveys, the protector over the land. Like the lion over the Jungle, "don't sleep"; on the face of he who appears to be humble or to some seem weak.

Welcome to life king of nature. Strong - and without your masculinity, there would be no peacemaker. Humbling to the thoughts of creation, strengthening the foundation, weathering the storm of human nature. We choose you; love you and honor your existence. Your position is threatening to many, your dominance has to be tested, the protector of the strength of all the nations you're going to be detested. Your quality is us sharing life's form with you, we're guided by your truth, we desire you. Precious creations, rather you're aware you fathered all the nations.

In history you've been downhill beaten; mistreated, it's time you stand in your position because your strength is really needed. Please feed us; with your spirit of comfort; too long it's been missing, now the children have fallen with the problem of not having your proper rearing. It might seem crazy, but it takes a village to do it, and your strength has been truly proven; to be needed, we're ready to eat it.

Man, of culture let me give you something, I don't like to use the word too loosely because it's overrated, but a King you truly are and too often you go unappreciated. Some people are too lax with making sure it's being stated. Should I take a moment to stroke the ego, are you comfortable enough to accept it? Don't take it too personal a woman carries a heavy day in her thoughts so you might often feel neglected, but you should never take it the way you often do because you are deeply respected. Every dream is for the moment to be perfect, and that in your world you'd dream of having one of us cultured girls in it.

We're very strong but it's more a semblance for our own protection, and by others experience, we've shielded ourselves assuming at some point you would deprive us of your affection. Having too many desires, seeking the environment for different women, and if that's not enough you'd throw us to the wolves when you were finished. That's merely preparation, for the sake of our mental health and our personal protection. Often, we feel like foot mats instead of stools for the comfort of your being - when we wait for you to be better you just beat us down to seek out other races of women. While we wait with what seems to be patience - Never wanting to be finished, our wombs we dream of carrying the seed of you in it. For our sons and daughters to exemplify your features, and for you to desire to stand in the paint to be our sons' and our daughters' teachers. Part of the problem is too many of our Moorish blooded people focus too much on bogus histories and begin to neglect the face of their offspring's sharing too many of those awful tendencies.

We long for you to show your children your dedication, show them the man we found in you so that; that can be their motivation. Show our daughters so they won't feel drought-ed, looking for affection in the absence of over standing looking without self to find it. Out of us comes the nurturer that's what's deeply embedded, and if I haven't said it, we look to you to make us feel protected. At least that's what we've been taught was your position, communications being the biggest issue causes you not to be able to listen. Could it be out of fear that man digresses from his original intention - afraid that he doesn't have what it takes to be attentive?

So often we both feel disrespected, and we begin to miss the true reason for being a whole, we just seem to continue to lose it, and the flaring egos make it hard for us to defuse it. Often, we just continue to abuse each other, now the children have no father and a damaged Mother.

You can kill the Dreamer, but you can't kill the Dream
-    Dr. Martin Luther King Jr

www.ingramcontent.com/pod-product-compliance
Lightning Source LLC
Chambersburg PA
CBHW041205180526
45172CB00006B/1199